Foreword by Amerigo Verardi
Afterword by Francesco Scatigna
Layout and Cover Design by Giovanni Capoccia e Luca Martelli
Edited in collaboration with the Subway Dharma Collective

Simon Chiatante

Floating Petals

流瓣

Subway Dharma Collective

For
Jiaomei Liu

CONTENTS

Being aware of the time passing, the breath of the wind blowing through the leaves of a mimosa before it strokes your hair, the fluttering wings of a sparrow which observes you through the crack in a wall while you're taking a sip of tea.

It is possible to deeply enjoy every aspect and every moment of life. But you should have lived it, first. You should have experienced also its darkest corners. And even after that, no one can guarantee that you'll be able to transform your conscience into the gift of Art.

In the pages of this book, poetry is at its purest, and it displays a deep sensitivity without ostentation. The author's capacity to blend in his verses very distant cultures comes primarily from his travels, and from his experiencing ways of living and of thinking that are almost opposite to one another. The subtle inquietude of a slow decadence in Western tints dilutes in the candor of an Eastern dawn and flourishes in pages of ink on rice paper. Words kowtow to the sublime perfection of nature's planes, even to the most delicate and invisible, and in the silence and contemplation generate new flowers, harmony, reflection, mindfulness, grace.

Taking a teaspoon of time to sip Simon Chiatante's poems is like meditating.

Amerigo Verardi

Along riversides and foothills
On the grasslands and barren cliffs
On top of all the withering stems
Only these floating petals.

CHAPTER 1

In reflection of far distances
Nel riflesso di grandi distanze

Oltre il cortile
Si stagliano le querce,

A ridosso del muro
Un giovane banyan
Sogna di origini remote.

Large oaks
Loom beyond the backyard,

A small banyan
Against the whitewash
Is dreaming of remote origins.

Sui tramonti d'oro di Pechino,
Sopra la polvere e le folle
Sospesi, sopra i tetti e sulle porte,
Su quelle vie, da noi un tempo percorse.

Over those golden sunsets in Beijing,
Over wild crowds and dusty ways,
Floating over roofs and over gates,
Over our walks in the old days.

A Kunming,

In un antico cortile
Il vapore si svolge
Dalle ciotole della gente
E decori, sorrisi
Sbocciano tra i graticci.

Kunming,

In an ancient courtyard
Smoke unfolding
From the people's bowls
Smiles and patterns
Blooming across the lattice.

Verità in un villaggio
Al riparo di basse nuvole.

Il martellare ritmico di un artigiano,
Bambini che giocano
Sotto la pioggia picchiante
Risate sparse
Sotto gocciolanti gronde,
Sfrecciano motorini
Veloci sulla pietra.

Truth in a village
Shadowed by low clouds.

The rhythmic hammering of an artisan,
Children playing
In the pattering rain
Sparse laughter
Under dripping eaves,
Speeding bikes
Rattle on the stone.

Svolazzano i mantra
Come onde infinite,

Echeggiano sui colli le eterne preghiere, i colori
Sono araldi degli eterni fiori.

Fretting mantras
Waving eternal,

Each bears the colours of a hundred flowers
While the cliff echoes with unending prayers.

Verdi monti di nebbia
Brezza sul lago

Opalescente
Battito d'ali
Mi esita intorno alle mani.

Green misty mountains
Breeze by the lake

Silk opalescence
Flutters its wings
And wavers, direct to my hands.

Rovine sul Dumyat
Coperte di muschio,
Vecchie tracce coperte di felci,
Ed ora
Che scorrono i ricordi
Non vedo più le nostre colline.

Moss-covered ruins
Over Dumyat,
Ferns have covered our foot-paths,
And now
That I'm drifting in memories
Our hills can no longer be seen.

Solo, su un confine
Dove bianche vastità
Rispondono
Di tutti
Emerge un tronco solitario
Che canta del proprio declino:
'Non c'è spazio per negare'

Cieco è il suono
Della nostra interna vastità.

Left in a borderland
Where the white vastness
Answers
For all of you
A solitary emergent tree
Flings its voice of decay:
'There's no space for denial'

Blind is the sound
Of our inner vastness.

Quel loto nascosto
Fiamma azzurra nel lago
Non potremmo mai toccarlo.

That secret lotus
A blue flame in the steamy lake
Our hands will never hold it.

Turchese
Le prime ore del giorno
Diluiscono i sogni.

Turquoise
Daybreak comes
Diluting dreams.

Bagliore
Interno alla città
Una mimosa in fiore.

Glow, encrypted
Through the city,
Mimosa in bloom.

Bocche di lupo
Divagano insieme
Sui muri.

Snapdragons
Assemble erratic
Against the walls.

Gazze che chiacchierano
Non è per niente
Se le ascolti.

Magpies' chatter
It's no background
If you listen.

Storie del cielo
E d'immortali, nel presente
Di una mosca.

In the still present, a fly
Recounts stories
Of heavens and immortals.

Fulgenti pianure,
Le inessenzialità spazzate via
Da venti ostinati.

Blazing flatlands,
Sweeping nonnecessities,
An obstinate wind.

Certezze inosservate,
Come ti chiamano
Passero audace?

Unseen certainties,
What do they call you
Brave bird?

Un lento gigante
Risponde al suo ciclico mandato
La luna cremisi.

A crawling giant
Answering to its cyclic call,
The crimson moon.

Scintillano lame nella notte,
I danzatori della fluida corrente
Domano la loro anima.

Gleaming blades in the night,
Dancers of the flowing stream
Are taming their souls.

Restando saldi
Accanto a deboli radici
e i venti dell'Est.

Standing
Grounded, beside withered roots
Eastern winds.

Spazzati pian piano
E senza attenzione
Discorsi si allineano
Coi muri d'orizzonte.

Slowly blown
In forgetfulness
Discourses align
With high-walled still horizons.

Onde serene
Riposano a riva

Prati selvatici
Tremano.

Waves placid
Rest ashore

Wild meadows
Vibrate.

Raffiche dal nord
Dal mare
Sorge la luna.

Northern gale
Offshore
Rises the moon.

Quali erano le tue parole?
Andate, come stormi migratori
Non torneranno più.

What were your words?
They left like migrating flocks
And they won't return.

Placidi canneti
ondeggiano
quali memorie.

Placid bamboo groves
Wave like
Memories.

CHAPTER 2

In a cup of tea
In una tazza di tè

In un mondo generato
Da una bolla nell'acqua
La verità non potrebbe nascondersi
In una tazza insapore di tè?

In a world
Created from a water bubble
Can't the truth be found
In a flavourless cup of tea?

Piove
Inclinata
La tiepida luce d'estate
Attraversa la sala da tè.

The rain falling
Tilted
Tepid summer light
Pervades the tranquil teahouse.

Osservi da sola
La notte scintillare

Ma la patinata argilla e gli utensili consunti
Profumano ancora
Della nostra ultima infusione
Tempo fa...

Watching the gleaming skyline
All alone tonight

But the dull clay and unpolished bamboo
Are still fragrant
With our last brew
Long ago…

Felicità e sofferenza
Non sono proprietà individuali.
Una volta lo imparammo
Di fronte a un semplice Tie Guan Yin, insieme.

Suffering and happiness
Are not only your own.
Once, we realised as much
In a casual Tie Guan Yin together.

Sopra una vetta scozzese
Pendii boscosi

Le rose di maggio
Si affacciano sulla città
Celebrando con grazia Orientale.

On a Scottish peak
Forest slopes

Roses of May
Overlooking town
Celebrate with Eastern beauty.

La biblioteca
Ormai vuota da ore.

Il cielo ricopre le colline
Con un manto di prugna,
E in queste latitudini
È meglio non chiedere mai l'ora.

Una fiasca di tè caldo
Ci tiene svegli
Per tutta la notte.

For hours now
The library's been empty.

The sky looms
Burnished prune above the hills,
On these latitudes
Don't ask about the time.

A big, warm flask of tea
Keeps us awake
All night.

Sedendo con gli Otto Immortali
La mia mente vacilla
Tra la loro pazienza
E le mie ansie.

Ma aspirando a quelle vette
Sulle Montagne della Fenice
Percepisco questa tazza e mi risveglio
Accanto al lago di Tian Chi

Come una lucertola nera
Che osserva pacifica
Il mondo sottostante.

Sitting with the Eight Immortals
My mind bounces
Between their patience
And my worries.

But aspiring to those peaks
Upon the Phoenix Mountains
I sense the cup and awake
beside the Tian Chi lake

Like a black lizard
Looking placid
To the world below.

Tardive plumerie di rugiada
Neve esigua
Vortica nell'aria

Questa limpida tazza dorata
Si abbina alla mezza primavera
Mentre io penso all'autunno di Wu Dong.

Dew-damp late plumerias
Snowflakes, few
Swirl airborne

This clear golden cup
Matches mid-spring
But I'm thinking of Autumn in Wu Dong.

Tè, riso
In mezzo alle nuvole.
Si nutre il se in semplicità,
L'acqua ravvivata su fiamme vivaci.

Un attimo lontano dalla frenesia
In uno studio di Chaoshan
Dove stima e ammirazione
Sono sempre ripagate da un fresco infuso.

Tea, rice
Amidst the clouds.
Nourishing the self in simplicity
Water is kept alive on lively fire.

A moment from the bustle
In a Chaoshan studio
Where esteem and appreciation
Is always repaid with a fresh brew.

Marciapiedi muti,
La città matura
Auroree magnolie.

Sidewalks, silent
The town's ripened
Dawny magnolias.

Onde di erba,
Il grano in autunno
Gioca alla primavera.

Waves of grass,
The wheat in autumn
Playing spring.

Miele selvatico
Pesche mature,
In ombra sotto gli alberi di mango
Si scorrono strade a mezzogiorno.

Honey wild
Ripe peaches,
Shaded in mango trees
Run late noon avenues.

In silenzio, nostalgia
Al riparo da una tempesta
Sorseggio miele ed orchidee.

Silent longing
Sheltered from the storm
I sip Honey Orchids.

Rovi intrecciati
Con la menta, respirano
Lungo un sentiero nascosto.

Mint-matted brambles
Breathe across
A long-forgotten pathway.

Jujube e frutta secca
Dalla natura selvaggia
Una giovane gru si rinfresca sulla riva.

Jujube and dry berries
From the wild
A young crane washes on the shore.

Integrata ormai
Nell mio stesso flusso vitale
Una voce automatica
'il bagno è pronto.'

Ma l'acqua?

Embedded
In my own life flow
An automatic voice
"the bath is ready"

But what about the water?

Un piano in lontananza,
Gialla e tranquilla coccinella
Attraversa lentamente il cortile.

Piano in the distance,
A slow mellow yellow
Ladybug across the yard.

Da un vicolo nascosto
In un angolo della città
'beviti una tazza di tè.'

From a hidden side-alley
"have a cup of tea"
Within the city hassle.

Via verso il mondo
La giovane maestra Wang
Partì da casa per la capitale.

La troverai purificare
La città in fermento
Nell'elegante argilla di Yixing.

Out to see the world
Young master Wang left home
For the capital.

You'll find her
Rinsing the fermenting city
Through the elegance of Yixing clay.

Trasportando con maestria
La natura selvaggia, le curvature
Delle torri di Shenzhen
Nell'argilla dorata, un tamburo ed un cappello di paglia.

Il maestro Sun mi ha fornito
Una teiera di Huang Yilong
- proteggiti dal pulviscolo del mondo -

Coaxing out the wildlife
On his golden clay, and the soft
Shenzhen towers
On a round drum lidded with a straw hat.

Master Sun provided me
With a pot of Huang Yilong
- Protect yourself from the dust of this world -

Una castagna
Come tazza;
Si bolle il tè sopra il fuoco,

Dall'Hubei fino al Gobi
Ti servono le forze
Per piantare nel deserto.

Hollow chestnut
As a cup;
Boiling brick tea on a stove,

From Hubei to the Gobi
You need to keep vigorous
Planting trees in the desert.

Vette verdi pattugliano nel sud,
preziose sorgenti da una cava.

Destrezza ed eleganza,
Nessuna goccia fuori posto
Dal Gaiwan, riverso come il destino

Donne Hakka
Preparano il raccolto
Di dolci tè verdi e del famoso Nove.

Green peaks patrolling the South,
Precious springs from a cave.

Straight pose, swift wrist
No spilling from the Gaiwan
Turning like the destiny of mankind.

Ladies of Hakka
Are preparing their soft harvest
Of greens and famous Number Nine.

Spesso al limitare
Dei rimpianti
Torno qui

Facendo sì che questa tazza
Risciacqui le mie ansie.

Often on the verge
Of past regrets
I come back here.

letting this cup of tea
Wash my cares away.

Fluidità ed essenza,
In moto gli elementi
Rimano tra la tazza ed il sé.

Fluency and essence,
The elements in motion
Rhyme between the cup and the self.

Cosa vedrai
Nel riflesso in una goccia
Di rugiada?

What will you see
In the reflection
Of a dewdrop?

Coralli
Multicolore in un abisso,

Il sole attraversa
Questo tè per tessere
Un broccato cantastorie.

Multi-coloured
Corals in a black sea,

The sun shines through
This tea like a storytelling
Brocade.

Vaniglia calar del sole
Paesani togati di nero
Si curano di antichi alberi
Dopo nevi propizie.

Vanilla sundown
Black-robed villagers
Nurturing old trees
After auspicious snowfalls.

Anche dal dorso
Di un'aquila divina
Si notarono i germogli
Degli alberi di Tai
Per il loro squillo acuto.

Even riding
On the back of a fairy eagle
You could spot the buds
Of the Tai trees
By their potent shrill.

Nascoste nella dolce nebbia
Di qualche cima remota
Le bandiere del Re degli uccelli
Scacciano i demoni del sonno.

From the summits,
Hidden in sweet mist
Bird King banners
Banish slumber demons.

Sotto cupole notturne
Di fiori d'arancio
Api cosmiche producono
Il loro miele secolare
Sottoforma di alberi.

Una foresta segreta
Che solo un cane inquieto troverebbe.

In nocturnal canopies
Of orange blossoms
Cosmic bees have harvested
Their honey
In the form of ancient trees.

A hidden forest
Only a mad dog could find.

Boschetti
Di pini sempreverdi
Sospirano –

Una tazza di verde Tai.

Evergreen
Pine groves
Simmer in the heat –

A cup of wild green Tai.

Ondeggiano I bambù
Ai venti d'occidente
Destandosi coi rovi e con i giunchi.

Bamboo bent
Under West winds
Awaken with reeds and brambles.

Sospiri d'argento
– rime ricamate dalla luna
Sulla foresta.

Silver whispers –
Moon-embroidered rhymes
Within the forest.

Il soffio della montagna
Si dissolve
Nei cieli di ghiaccio.

Breath of the mountain
Dissolving through
The frozen skies.

Distratto
Dalle cicale
– tutto il tè sulla scrivania.

Cicadas
Distracted me –
Tea all over my desk.

In giro col mio thermos
Da un luogo all'altro,
Le stelle mi conoscono,
Sempre lo stesso ragazzo
Ma più brizzolato.

Carrying my flask around
From place to place,
The stars have witnessed
The same tea boy
Turning white.

Vecchie tazze incrinate
E una matita

Nel caso in cui
Queste note amare, diluite nel ricordo,
Cospirino con ombra e rifrazione.

Old cracked vessels
And a pencil

On the off chance that
These bitter notes, softened by memory,
May conspire with shades and refraction.

Stridono cicale
In una tazza di tè
C'è un volto?

Cicadas' trill –
In a cup of tea
Whose face?

CHAPTER 3

Anticipations of dawn
Previsioni d'aurora

Tacito portale
Adesso
Brezze sui frangenti d'indaco

Un ventaglio sui capelli.

Silent gate
Suchness
Blowing on the waves of indigo

Like a fan in my hair.

Piume di vermiglio
Irradiano
Le lande

Aprendosi ferite nelle ombre,
Nel tragitto contro il cielo.

Vermillion
Feathers propagate
Across the land,

Gauging their wounds in each shadow
Follow their path against the sky.

Sfidando la tempesta
Sulla costa.

Cacciata o accompagnata
Da una bianca tigre
In agguato.

Defying the storm
Along the coast.

Chased or accompanied
By a white tiger
Crouched.

Nell'immergere le mani in uno stagno
Ho toccato le fredde
stelle immortali.

Una tartaruga in lotta con una serpe,
L'ho visto cento volte nei miei sogni
L'ho visto cento volte tra i torrenti.

Plunging my hands into a pond
I touched the still
Immortal stars.

A turtle wrestling with a snake,
I've seen it in a hundred dreams
I've seen it near a hundred streams.

Tracciando un pellegrinaggio
Per invisibili città, un drago azzurro

Difficile da discernere
Dalle sue spettrali cave.

Trailing its pilgrimage in invisible cities,
An azure drake

That's hard to discern
From its ghostly cave.

Lucente broccato,
Maree respirano
Sulla nostra testa.

Blazing brocade,
Overlayered breath
Above our heads.

Ali d'argento
Scalfiscono
Un campo vuoto.

Argentine wings
Emblazoning
An empty field.

Giunchi liberi
Slegati in acquitrini

Libera
Spettrale
Vacuità.

Free reeds
Untied in the marshes

Free
Empty
Shadows.

Nella notte torbida del caos

Come pipistrelli nel proprio regno
Si perdono confusi luce e oscurità

Dove non esiste impermanenza.

Shambles of the cloudy night.

Light and darkness are lost
In the haphazard realm of bats

No place for impermanence.

La luna racchiude
Con passo solenne
L'alba ed il tramonto.

With solemn pace
the Moon
encloses dusk and dawn.

Un portale solitario
Presiede
La rotazione del cielo.

The turning sky
Presided
By a single gate.

In tempesta
Ruggisce un drago convulso

Si estendono
Drappi di luce.

In downpours
Roars a writhing dragon

Banners of expanding
Light.

Segui ruscelli rocciosi
Tra i boccioli del pesco,

Il Re degli uccelli
Riaccende il suo richiamo
Nelle braci di carbone.

Follow rocky rivulets
Amidst peach blossoms,

The King of birds
Rekindling its call
In charcoal embers.

Potrai mai afferrare
I baffi di una tigre?
Potrai mai afferrare
I corsi di un ruscello?

Chiudi quel rubinetto.

Can you grab
A tiger's whiskers?
Can you grab
A forest's brook?

Close that tap.

One fish muddies the water,
Imagine six!

But they're still free
Within their own nature.

Un pesce annebbia le acque,
Immagina sei!

Liberi comunque
Nella loro intrinseca natura.

Nessuna aquila è abbattuta
Da una freccia di secoli fa
- umida brezza.

Felled no eagle,
An arrow shot eons ago
- fresh moist breeze.

Lo stagno profondo, sepolto
Grano vivo, quasi maturo
S'intreccia verso oriente.

A deep pool buried,
Vibrant wheat about to ripen
Weaving eastwards.

Rugiada amara d'autunno
I sogni e la foschia
Pervadono l'alba di mistero.

Bitter dew in fall,
Turbid haze and dreams
Pervade and mystify the dawn.

Oltre oceani,
Enormi distanze.

Tenendo un ventaglio
Di rovi già sepolti
Molto in basso.

Across the oceans,
In great distances.

Holding a fan
Of brambles already
Several yards beneath.

Le stelle sono i misteri del mondo,
Mattoni di un santuario abbandonato
E i ricordi
Riflessi nella pioggia.

Stars are mysteries of the world
Like the bricks of a forgotten shrine
And memories
Reflected in the raindrops.

E nel silenzio
Bianco come la seta
Il solo fruscio di una veste,

Una stilla dorata
Gocciola da un vaso

Versata
Nel vasto mare
Della sofferenza.

And in the silence
White as a silken cloud
The mere swish of a robe,

A golden tear
Tinkles from a jar

Dropping
In the vast sea
Of sorrow.

Passo dopo passo
Sono
Già qui,

Solida
Come la libertà
La mia casa
È in ogni respiro.

Step after step
I am already here,

Solid
Like freedom
My home
Is every breath.

Guardando la luna calante
Preparo la penna
Per scrivere nulla.

Looking at the setting moon
I take my pen to write –
There's nothing to write.

Lungo le rive e sotto i colli
Sopra i prati e i monti aspri
Sopra tutti gli steli appassiti
Solo questi petali sospesi.

Place yourself at the middle of a crossroad, if you dare defy the incoming traffic. You may then just see a bundle of uninteresting concrete paths that, having carved their ways through the city, will then deliver their burden of vehicles to their uninteresting destinations. Perhaps it depends on the days, or the mood, or the weather – you may see something else instead: a bundled series of alternative paths, each one bearing its own singularity as a rising standard, each one jealous of its own prerogatives and destination.

Yet you are not taking any of these roads; you are merely standing at their crossing. What does that make you? Which road do you belong to?

Some people dislike standing at the crossroad – they perhaps take their time to choose which path to take, and then begin their journeys. That is all well for them. However, a few others do not want to decide: they behold all those paths, they would like a glimpse of all of them, or at least of some of them.

Let's cut the metaphor short. Some of us dislike the idea of being defined by their place of birth, or by their native language; not because we hate either of them, but because we feel we are not defined by them. Living and speaking and writing in multiple languages let us be what we long to be – our own individual selves, partaking in communities and cultures and histories as wide ranging as we are prepared to allow our identities to stretch.

This collection is one of those crossroads. It blends cultures, perspectives, art forms that do not often mingle. It wants not to be defined, but merely to communicate. It

manages its complex identity through simplicity, imme-
diacy, relatability. It is not meant to be a dissertation on
how to be oneself: it is an expression of an individual's
journey within its own complexity, fragility, doubts.

Anyone's journey is purely his or her own; and that one
would share his cannot be welcomed other than by a deep
feeling of gratefulness and heartwarming wonder.

Francesco Scatigna

Made in the USA
Columbia, SC
22 August 2022

65852835R00109